Teacher

Published in the United States of America by Cherry Lake Publishing
Ann Arbor, Michigan
www.cherrylakepublishing.com

Reading Adviser: Marla Conn MS, Ed., Literacy specialist, Read-Ability, Inc.
Book Design: Jennifer Wahi
Illustrator: Jeff Bane

Photo Credits: © Tatiana Frank / Shutterstock.com, 5; © wavebreakmedia / Shutterstock.com, 7, 15; © antoniodiaz / Shutterstock.com, 9; © Monkey Business Images / Shutterstock.com, 11, 19; © SpeedKingz / Shutterstock.com, 13; © mariakraynova / Shutterstock.com, 17; © michaeljung / Shutterstock.com, 21; © India Picture / Shutterstock.com, 23; © aleksandr-mansurov-ru, 2-3, 24; Cover, 1, 6, 8, 18, Jeff Bane

Library of Congress Cataloging-in-Publication Data

Names: Bell, Samantha, author.
Title: Teacher / Samantha Bell.
Description: Ann Arbor, Michigan : Cherry Lake Publishing, [2017] | Series:
   My Friendly Neighborhood | Audience: Grades: K to Grade 3.
Identifiers: LCCN 2016056586| ISBN 9781634728287 (hardcover) | ISBN
   9781634729178 (pdf) | ISBN 9781534100060 (paperback) | ISBN 9781534100954
   (hosted ebook)
Subjects: LCSH: Teachers--Juvenile literature.
Classification: LCC LB1775 .B435 2018 | DDC 371.102--dc23
LC record available at https://lccn.loc.gov/2016056586

Printed in the United States of America
Corporate Graphics

About the author: Samantha Bell has written and illustrated over 60 books for children. She lives in South Carolina with her family and pets. She is very thankful for the helpers in her community.

About the illustrator: Jeff Bane and his two business partners own a studio along the American River in Folsom, California, home of the 1849 Gold Rush. When Jeff's not sketching or illustrating for clients, he's either swimming or kayaking in the river to relax.

Teachers help students learn new things.

They plan the **lessons**. They grade the tests.

Some teachers teach more than one subject. Some teach only one.

What is your teacher's name?

Some teach art. They show the class how to draw and paint.

Some teach students how to play an **instrument**. Some play the piano. Some play the drums.

Some teach **drama**. The students put on plays.

Some are **P.E.** teachers.
They show the class how to
exercise.

What is your favorite class?

Teachers show students new things. They take them to new places. They plan field trips.

Some teachers are coaches.
They show students how to play
on a sports team.

Teachers listen. They solve problems. They want students to do well.

Teachers are ready to help.
They make learning fun.

What would you like to ask a teacher?

glossary

drama (DRAH-muh) the subject or practice of acting

instrument (IN-struh-muhnt) something used to make music

lessons (LES-uhns) assignments or exercises

P.E. (PEE-EE) physical education

index